A Dog's Life

Poetry by Jan Garrod

Whiteley Publishing

© Jan Garrod 2013

All rights reserved. No part of this book may be reproduced or transmitted in any form by any means, electronic or mechanical, including photocopying, recording, or by any information storage and retrieval system without written permission of the publisher, except where permitted by law.

Published by Whiteley Publishing Ltd
First paperback edition 2013

ISBN 978-1-908586-42-1

Jan Garrod has asserted her right under the Copyright, Designs and Patents Act 1988, to be identified as the author of this work.

A Dog's Life

Splashing around and rolling in mud,
Eating cow dung is pretty good.
Bursting a ball and fetching sticks,
Giving my owner lots of licks.

Digging up the garden and chewing a bone,
But I really don't like being left alone.
Chasing the cat who lives next door,
Leaving paw marks on a nice clean floor!

Helping my owner finish their tea,
These are the things that matter to me.
Looking out the window and having a bark,
Going for a walk, in the local park.

Running around the garden having a play,
Going to bed on a cold, rainy day.
Making a fuss of people I've just met,
But I really don't like a trip to the vet!
These are the things that I like the most,
Oh! Don't forget tearing up the post!

A Doggy Can't Help It!

It's not my fault, the biscuits were there,
They looked so good, I thought you'd share.
But from the tone of your voice, I think I was wrong,
So I don't think I'm hanging around here for long.

I'm going for a walk, but I won't go too far,
For I might try my luck, with that chocolate bar.

A Walk in the Park

They took me for a ride in the car today,
Normally I'm not keen, I have to say.
It usually ends up with a trip to the vet's,
And that's as good as it possibly gets.
But not today, we went to a park,
Where I saw some dogs and had a bark.

I got ticked off, but it was really good,
I'd have chased a bitch, if only I could.
She was real cute and smelt just right,
I'd give her a hump, if I got her in sight.
But I couldn't do anything, I was on my lead,
My owners think it's something I need.
But I'd be fine, on my own for a while,
This stupid lead, it cramps my style.

Alone With a Bone

Mistress is going out she's painting her face,
She'll be off chasing rabbits all over the place.
Up and down hills and running through the grass,
While I'm stuck at home, just sat on my ass.

Mistress calls it work, but I think it's play,
She really must like it, 'cause she goes everyday.
It's not that fair when she leaves me all alone,
And all I have for company is a smelly, old bone!

Bye Bye Cat

The alarm went off, but nobody heard,
Now they're dashing around without a word.

They're all running late, there's no time for my fuss,
The only good thing is there was none for the puss!
She's gone off in a huff I hope she's moved out,
We could manage quite well, without her about.

Call that a Spider!

I was fast asleep when my Mistress screamed,
At first I thought it was something I dreamed.
She was in the bathroom so I went up to see,
leaving the comfort of my nice, warm settee.
I couldn't believe it when I finally saw,
The tiny spider climbing up the door.

The way she screamed I thought it was large,
And she needed me to come and take charge.
So, I'll leave her alone to sort out the beast,
I'm off to the kitchen to have me a feast.
I saw some biscuits left out on the table,
And they had my name written on the label.

Come Home Soon

My owner should be back anytime now,
I just know this, don't ask me how.

I can't tell the time, but I know that she's due,
It's my rumbling tummy that gives me a clue.

For when she gets home, she opens some tins,
Then mistress and me, we have our dins.

Digging for Victory

I'm in trouble 'cause I dug a little hole,
Mistress asked me if I was excavating for coal.
She doesn't sound happy, she sounds a little stroppy,
Something to do with uprooting a poppy.

A plant looks like a weed, if you know what I mean
To a terrier like me, it's another bit of green.
But I'll leave the plants alone, for what it's worth,
Any future digging will be done in bare earth!

Doggy Heaven

I've been in the field and rolled in mud,
Chased many birds as fast as I could.
Splashed in the pond and eaten some dirt,
Got muddy spots on my owner's new shirt.

Foraged in the undergrowth and found a vole,
Started digging a really good hole.
But now we're back I haven't a care,
So give me a drink and vacate that chair.

Doggy's Day Out

Someone was in a hurry and forgot to close the gate,
So I went down the lane to the bitch at number eight.
I was just about to hump her as a voice cut through the air,
Get out of here you mangy dog, find your fun elsewhere!

But the day wasn't lost, there was still number two,
Though when I got there, there was actually a queue.
The bitch who lives there, she must be on heat,
Three dogs in the yard and one on the street!

I wasn't about to queue, or stand around and wait,
I thought I'd go home and sneak back in the gate.
It must be about time to help my mistress with her toast,
And have a good bark at the man who brings the post.

Doin' the Tile Dance

Today, I achieved a personal best,
Although my owner wasn't impressed.

She'd just mopped the floor, it was nice and clean,
My feet were muddy, if you see what I mean.

I did a little dance and got every tile,
Which made paddling in mud, really worthwhile.

I'm now in the doghouse and she's fussing the cat,
And I'll tell you now, I'm not happy about that!
But given half a chance, I'll do it again,
I'll be outside in the morning, hoping for rain.

Feed Me!

She's picked up my bowl, and she's got the tin,
Now I'm just waiting for her to put something in.

But she's stopped for a chat, with that thing to her ear,
Now I'll never get my food, of that I fear.

I haven't been fed, for an hour or more,
And I want my food, of that I'm sure.

So put that thing down and get on with my dinner,
Cos minute by minute, I'm stood here getting thinner!

Get a Move On!

I'm stood at the door, I need to go out,
But when you need someone, they're never about.

If they don't hurry up, there's gonna be a puddle,
Then I won't stand a chance of getting a cuddle.

So please get a move on and open this door,
Or bring that mop, you'll need it for sure!

Get Him!

I'm going to get the postman, if it's the last thing that I do.
There's a hole in the door, that he pushes things through.

I don't know why he bothers, 'cause I'll rip them all up.
Though I'm always told off and told I'm not a little pup.

But it's in my job description, that I have to guard the pack.

So when that postman comes again, his fingers I'll have for a snack.

Glorious Mud!

That was a good walk, everywhere was mud,
I ran in it and rolled in it, like a terrier should.

My belly is dripping, in water that's black,
That'll need drying, when we get back.

There's mud in my paws, I can feel it for sure,
That's gonna be fun on her nice, clean white floor.

Now it's time for a shake, just watch them run,
This is a terrier's idea of having fun!

Goodbye Cat!

I want to sit on your knee, but the cat's sat there,
Looking all high and mighty, the great ball of fur.
She doesn't love you like I do, that's for sure,
You should make her get off and sit on the floor.

She won't lick your hand, or bring you a stone,
She won't guard the house, or leave you a bone.
She only needs a bed and food on demand,
And the rest of the time, she's very offhand.

So mistress dear, I think you'll agree,
You're much better off with me on your knee.
Just give me the word and I'll tell her to scat,
I don't understand why we need to have a cat!

Hand Over the Cake!

Surely you won't eat all that cake,
You'll make yourself sick, for goodness sake?
If you need some help, I'm ready and able,
So pass it down from off the table.

It'll help your diet, if you give it to me,
You'll be super slim, just wait and see.
Then when we go on our usual walk,
The man with the Yorkie might stop to talk.

You'll become good friends and go on a date,
And all because I helped you, lose weight!

I Hate ALL Cats!

I was fast asleep when I heard the shout,
We're going for a walk, do you want to go out.
Of course I do, I'm a dog you know,
So get my lead and hurry let's go.

Are we going to the shop to buy me a treat,
Or off to the butchers to get me some meat?
There's always the park and I could have me a run,
You can look at flowers, that'll be fun.

We could visit your friend, with the Labrador bitch,
She has a cold nose, with a cute little twitch.
Then there's the pet shop, I quite fancy a bone,
Or a walk in the field and I'll find me a stone.
But when I hear where you're going, I'm not too keen,
And when I tell you, you'll see what I mean.

My mistress's friend, she has a new cat,
And would you believe, we're going to see that.
If I'd have known, I'd have stayed in bed,
And dreamed about chasing a cat instead!

I Hate That Cat!

I hate that cat, with her knowing look,
Like she's read the contents of an encyclopaedia book.
She thinks she's so clever, but just watch and wait,
I'll have her next time, before she makes that gate.

She stays out all night, that stupid, silly cat,
Can't see my owner ever letting me do that.
Then she sits on the newspaper and nothing is said,
If I did that, I'd be told off instead.

When I disturbed her, she hissed and spat,
I'm bigger than her, I'm not frightened of that.
But I've got my revenge, my plan was smooth as silk,
For while she was out, I drank all her milk!

I Hate That Cat!!!

Today, it was nearly world war three,
When I caught that cat eating my tea.
I chased her out the room and up the stairs,
Twice round the table and under the chairs.

She hid behind the sofa, but I sniffed her out,
There's no escaping my super, sensitive snout!
So she ran in the garden and climbed up a tree,
Faster than a car in the Monaco Grand Prix!

Now an hour has passed and she's not down yet,
And it's started to rain, she's going to get wet!
So a soggy, moggy she's going to be,
That's punishment enough, for eating my tea.

I Still Hate That Cat!

I stood at the door because I wanted to go out,
Now I want to come in and there's no one about.
I bet they're inside eating something nice,
While I'm out here, frozen like ice.

I don't think it's right that the cat gets a door,
My guarding duties I think I'll withdraw.
I'll have a good bark, that'll bring them running,
How's about that for terrier cunning?

I'll Do the Cleaning

My owners are scoffing a late night treat,
Cheese and biscuits they like to eat.
So I stick close to lend a hand,
It's what dogs do if you understand.

My owner scolds me for sniffing around,
I'm just clearing up the crumbs to be found.
It's not my fault, you're messy when you eat,
And there's bits of food all around your feet.

Better they're eaten, than go to waste,
So move your feet and I'll do it in haste!

I'm in Trouble!

My owners due back and I'm in trouble,
Better practice my cute look on the double.
I had an accident and knocked over a vase,
It landed on my head and I saw stars.

Mistress won't be pleased, it was full of flowers,
I tried to put them back with my limited powers.
Picked them up in my mouth, but they tasted bad,
So I hope my mistress won't be too mad.

In the Doghouse

Mistress is moaning, I'm in her bad books,
Her voice is raised and I'm getting looks.
I didn't know it was her best dress,
And now she says it's a total mess.

It was very comfy and it smelt real nice,
After I shuffled it around, once or twice.
Now I'm banished to the floor, how sad is that?
Having to lie on an old piece of mat!

It's in The Job Description!

I have to beg for food whenever you eat,
Especially so if you're having meat.
I must chase cats I have no choice,
When they start meowing in that silly voice.
My nose should be cold, shiny and wet,
And stuck in every place it can possibly get.
At every given chance I must bark out loud,
Especially when we're out and in a crowd.

I should sleep on the bed it's only right,
When my owner's asleep, I sneak on in the night.
I must guard the pack from a passing stranger,
Keep them safe from any form of danger.

It's my duty to wreck the lawn,
Kill all the grass in any shape or form.
Dig up the garden and chuck out plants,
Turn a deaf ear when my owner rants.
If only once in the middle of the night,
Lick your owner to give them a fright.
But the number one thing you must keep in mind,
Is to get that postman and bite his behind!

It's Only Snow!

We were going for a walk, until she saw the snow,
Now she's changed her mind, but I want to go.

Gentle persuasion, that's all mistress should need,
To put on her coat and fetch my lead.

She's got those green things, to put on her feet,
She'll feel much better, after giving me a treat!

It's Snowing!

*Woke up this morning and looked out the door,
There was something white all over the floor.
It was cold to the touch and felt like ice,
But running around in it felt really nice.
It fell from the sky and tickled my nose,
And made my owner put on extra clothes.*

*The cat didn't like it and wouldn't go out,
So I gave her a nudge with the end of my snout.
It's now getting deep, but it's really good fun,
As I slip and slide, while I try hard to run.*

Mud is Good!

I don't want a bath, I'm not even dirty,
But if I play up, my mistress gets shirty.
"You're a smelly, hound; you've been rolling in mud."
You know I'd roll in manure, if only I could.
But she likes me clean and smelling all sweet,
So I'd better be good, or I won't get my treat.

My Friend Spike.

I found something strange in the garden, it was round and brown like a ball.
I've seen it run, but when you go near it, you can't see legs or head at all.

I like to find it and have a good sniff, but those spikes, really make me twitch.
It's covered in things that creep and crawl, goodness they do make me itch.

My pack leader shouts, "Leave it alone, you're going to get covered in fleas".
But it is my job to find these things, so let me get on with it, PLEASE!!!

My Views on Water.

Water is good when you need a drink,
Tastes even better out of the sink.
I like to splash in a babbling brook,
I think my coat really suits the wet look.

A day at the beach, to swim in the sea,
It's really good fun, I think you'd agree.
A muddy puddle is good for a laugh,
the only water I hate is when it's a BATH!

Never Did Like That Collar!!!

"Where's your collar?" I hear my owner shout.
Well it was round my neck before I went out.
It might have fell off when I was chasing the cat,
Collars that are loose can often do that.

Perhaps it was when I was digging in the flowers,
I was doing that for hours and hours.
It could have been when I went through the hedge,
To have a run around in next doors veg.

Hey! Now I remember it's in the cabbage patch,
That's where it fell off while I was having a scratch!

Oh No! I've got a Friend

Why do you keep on scratching? My mistress said to me.
Well I think that's pretty obvious, I'm sure I've got a flea.
I bet it's from the hedgehog, that I sniff out everyday.
Hold the nose, close the eyes, Here comes that dreadful spray.

One Cluck Too Much!

I'm watching you chicken,
With your cluck, cluck, cluck
Scratching round all day,
In all that muck, muck, muck

Me, I'm just waiting
For the faintest chance,
Then you know what,
We'll see such a merry, little dance.

You think you're really so clever,
Because you can lay an egg,
But I'm really looking forward,
To perhaps trying a chicken leg!

OOPS!

I'm back in the dog house, I've been eating some "Goo",
But when it's lying there, what else can you do?
When you're a dog, it tastes really, very good,
You know, you ought to try it, you really should!

Prewash

I like it when, they open up the machine,
To put the dirty pots inside,
They do it after they've had some food,
I think those pots they're trying to hide.

Give me the chance to lick all those pots,
There's so much left to taste,
You know, it really is such a great shame,
To just let all that stuff go to waste.

Rescue Me, (Please)

How did I come to be in this cage?
I've been stuck in here for what seems like an age.
I look all innocent as the people pass by,
But they always seem to choose another dog nearby.
I always look happy and I wag my tail,
But it's like I'm hidden behind an invisible veil.

A little girl stops and gives me a smile,
And my hopes are raised, if only for a while.
But Mum and Dad, they shake their head,
And point to my neighbour, a pedigree instead.
My heart sinks, yet another night alone,
When the only thing I want is a nice new home.

I hide in the corner, I'm feeling very sad,
Then the girl re-appears followed by her Dad.
"I like this one", I hear her cry,
Her Mum and Dad frown and ask her why.
"He's really cute and looks like he's fun",
They could see from her face, her heart I'd won.
So I have my new home and a family who care,
And guess what? I even have my very own, comfy chair.

Resistance is Futile

I give my mistress my hypnotic stare,
As I peep out from under a chair.
You're eating some choc, I'd like some too,
Just remember who it is that really loves you.

She shakes her head, and says "It's mine",
But she ought to share, looking at her waistline.
She can't resist me, she gives me a square,
You see it always works, my hypnotic stare.

Roses For You, But Not for Me

She's done it again, that mistress of mine,
I love her dearly, I think she's divine.
But she puts on that spray with the awful smell,
Then pats my head, so I smell of it as well.

Dogs aroma should be of things gross and smelly,
Horrible things you pick up on your wellie.
Wee and goo and everything that's bad,
Can make a terrier's heart feel glad.

You can keep your perfumes, scents and roses,
They make us sneeze, when they get up our noses.
So I'll go in the garden and roll in some mud,
Then I'll start to smell like a real dog should!

Scaredy-Cat!

I crept up on the cat and gave her a fright,
She didn't see me come into sight.
She was fast asleep, lying in the chair,
So I barked in her ear and gave her a scare.

She leapt in the air, and ran from the room,
Then from the kitchen, I heard a voice boom.
"Leave the cat alone, you know she's not a toy,
There'll be no bones for you, naughty boy."

So as I pass the cat, I give her a mighty scowl,
Curl my lip and give a deep, little growl.
It's one up to the moggy, but my time will come,
When she's climbing the fence, I'll bite her bum!

Sharing is Good

I like to help my owner finish off their tea,
And if it's meat or chocolate, all the better for me.

Wouldn't want them to struggle with too much food,
That would be bad manners and extremely rude.
So sit by their side and fix them with a stare,
And they'll soon realise, there's plenty to share.

She Who Must Obey!

I've just been for a walk in the pouring rain,
Mistress wasn't too keen, she wished to abstain.
But it's only water at the end of the day,
So I gave her a look and she had to obey.

Mistress likes it hot when there's lots of sun,
But that's no good when you like to run.
A cooling shower or a gentle breeze,
Makes running around much more of a wheeze!

Smelly Hound!

You must be joking, you're having a laugh,
Saying I need another bath.
I only had one sometime last year,
And I don't want another, on that I'm clear!

I'm out of here, catch me if you can,
Dogs aren't supposed to smell like a man.
We're supposed to smell of goo and poo and wee,
That's what attracts all the bitches to me!

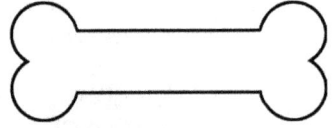

Sorry!

Mistress' sister, who's a little bit haughty,
Came to visit and I was really quite naughty!
I mounted her leg, excitement got the better,
Now I'm shut in the garden and it's getting wetter.

It's started to rain and they've forgotten about me,
They're far too busy drinking their tea.
I scratch at the door and hope they remember,
Don't want to be out here until the end of September!

Still Number One

Mistress is back and I'm absolutely agog,
When I went near her she smelt of dog.
And no! it's not me, I have to confess,
So this has put me under extreme duress.

She's been unfaithful with some other hound,
I drop my head and lie on the ground.

Mistress knows why and gives me a kiss,
And I soon realise she's still my Miss.
She might go places, other dogs to see,
But soon she comes back and it's me on her knee!

Terrier Beware!

That terrier down the road he keeps digging up my bones.
But he's in for a surprise, now I've buried some stones.

There's a hole in the hedge and he keeps sneaking through,
But if I catch him around, there'll be such a hulla-balloo.

That's my buried treasure for no-one else but me,
So he'd just better beware, that darned thieving escapee!

That'll Teach Her!

At last, you're back, come here and let me kiss ya,
Wet and slobbery to show how much I missed ya.
You were gone for hours, I thought you'd run away,
So to relieve the stress I had a little play.
For an hour or two, I had a good howl,
Then I had some fun, playing with the towel.

I raced around the house and chased my tail,
And oops, I'm sorry, I shredded the mail!
I knocked over a plant and broke the pot,
But don't worry about the soil, I ate the lot.

I growled at a salesman who came to the door,
And there's a puddle needs mopping on the kitchen floor.
When the cat popped in, I chased her round the house,
Now she knows how it feels to be a mouse!
I had a drink from the big, white bowl,
And tunnelled under the carpet, pretending to be a mole.

I've hidden your slipper and chewed on a shoe,
By then I was running out of things to do.
But apart from all that, I've been really good,
Just like any bored little terrier should.

Tick Tock Watch the Clock

I watch the clock 'til my mistress gets home,
Counting each minute, just like a metronome.
I howl when she leaves but it's to no avail,
I have to stay home and watch for the mail.

When she gets back, I'll have a little sulk,
I won't make a fuss, instead I'll just skulk.
But I can't keep it up when she gives me that smile,
I'll forgive her and be on her knee in a while.

Time for Bed

Hasn't my mistress seen the clock?
It's time we went to bed,
I've been waiting here many an hour,
But she's reading a book instead!

It's eleven thirty, it's really late,
And a terrier needs his sleep,
I need to be up bright and early,
Ready to herd any wayward sheep!

I'll dream of fields and rolling hills,
With dozens of rabbits to chase.
Then when I've shown them who's the boss,
Off home for my dinner I'll race.

Vet's Payback Day!!!

I'm sick of that vet, with his needles and pills,
When I'm pretty sure I don't have any ills!
But my owner takes me at least once a year,
Despite how much I'm shaking with fear.

I try for the door but my lead she pulls tight,
I'm dragged across the floor, with no dignity in sight.
The vet sticks things, where they really shouldn't be,
It's not very pleasant, I'm sure you'll agree.

He pokes and prods, then says I'm just fine,
Presents us with a bill, that's hardly benign.
Maybe next time I'll give him a bite,
Though I'm sure my owner will say, it's impolite!

Walkies

I've been out in the rain,
I'm absolutely soaking,
When mistress said "Walkies",
I thought she was joking.

Usually when it's raining,
She refuses to go,
And no chance of a walk,
If there's any sign of snow!

What! No Choc.

I heard the rustle of chocolate wrappers,
So I left my bed and ran like the clappers.
I am very partial to a little bit of choc,
but when I got there all I got was a shock.

All of it was gone, not one tiny bit left,
Talk about unhappy, I was totally bereft.
I'd share my doggy drops, even my bones,
And maybe one of my special stones.

So, back to bed where I'll dream about treats,
Where it's ME, ME, ME, that gets all of the sweets.

What's Christmas?

I can't believe what I've just seen,
There's a tree appeared, it's big and green.
It's in the house, it's not outside,
Just what they're doing, I can't decide.

There's things underneath, I like how they smell,
I think there's chocolate, I just can't tell.
It's Christmas, one of the little ones say,
So what is Christmas, at the end of the day?

But whatever it is, it smells real good,
And I'd like chocolate, I really would.
There's also something cooking, I think it's meat,
I hope there's some left for me to eat!

Where's the Tail?

Where's the tail that I'm supposed to wag?
I have my collar and my fancy tag.
But when I turn around and look at my rump,
All I have is a short, little stump!

My friend Rover's tail is really long,
What happened to mine? What went wrong?
Perhaps one day it might grow anew,
Then I can wag it, when I come to greet you!

www.ingramcontent.com/pod-product-compliance
Lightning Source LLC
Chambersburg PA
CBHW061253040426
42444CB00010B/2373